CALL ME THELMA

A collection of poems

Mary

Copyright © 2024 Mary Cox
All rights reserved
ISBN:

For my children and grandchildren.

Contents

Age	2
Hope	4
Listen	6
Clouds	8
The Bus Crash	10
Imprints	12
The Gorge	14
Mr. Rogers	16
Dad	18
Believe	20
Worth It	22
Silence	24
Interested	26
False Dedication	28
Dr. Neil's Garden	30
Difficult Wisdom	32
Edinburgh	34
Mean Girl	36

Contents

We Disappear	38
Self Reliance	40
Mom Said	42
First Love	44
When You Look	46
Minikhada	48
What If	50
Dad Again	52
Prayer	54
Sadness	56
Mother's Conversation	58
Solitude	60
We Search	62
Solo	64
Strength	66
Light	68
Welcom	70
Call Me Thelma	72

I've never been this age before.

Hope

She's everything to me
Said in passing
Whispered.

As if vapor from his soul escaped to assure that love is present.
Teaching hope without envy.

Certainty in the quiet din of the crowd.

Just believe.

Listen

Listen closely and you can feel
The howl of the wind as it hardens the air.

Dream of a place where cold ends the pain
The thirst for forgiveness denies all that is said.

Fear and freedom mix into one
The price of autonomy we didn't know we'd won.

Clouds

Moist touch of Heaven's breath
reaching from the sky to tough our cheeks and
envelope
our souls.

White and pure at times creating
fixtures of memories
forgotten in our rush for
the next experience.

Dark electric and shooting
ice seeds when provoked.
Echoing the passions and fears
suppressed by an imprisoned people.

Always returning hope
full of life giving water.

The Bus Crash

A routine day. Gearing up for slogging
Mixed with too much to do.

The bus crashed. We need nurses!

Chaos and fear turned into a team.
Looking to help in any way.

You were asleep. I chose to hold your head and
try to comfort, holding
Pressure to your bleeding as you started to wake.

How long have you lived in Oregon?
I'm here to help.
Breathe with me...slow, in and out.

Something happened you asked, did I do
something?
You will remember.
It is ok. Everyone is ok.

Let me hold your head.
Breathe with me again...slow, in and out.

Imprints

Imprints of emotion and remembrance
Hurt and love
What we recall at times seeps through our cells
As we breathe.

Wanted and unwanted scenes and
Feelings mixed with reality
And dreams.

I save a memory with a rock, song
Or t-shirt hoping the sense used will
Re-light the time of happiness.

Other memories intrude unwanted and triggered
When I am I sometimes unaware.

When I discover how to carry both
Trauma and happiness I will thrive.
Embody the past and present. But how.

The Gorge

Powerful water easing through the carved mountains
Healing from the unannounced fire, raw and scorched.

Mist then blue sunlight blown from the narrowed path the river created.

Life giving water feeding all who seek it.
Refilled from the sky, storms which drench the burnt hills
Causing the mountains to cry.

Mr. Rogers

Mr. Rogers lived across the street
In my childhood.
My best friend provided staunch caring as
We lived worry free
In our young dreams.

An unfractured two parent family
Appeared perfect
With trauma broken parents desperate
To provide normalcy.

Cinderella brainwashing to combat
Boot wearing reality.
Learned sacrifice and life
Opportunities provided hard knock
Lessons of my generation
Just as my parents had dreamed.

Dad

July 4th. Family celebration
Potato salad. Illegal fireworks.
Breakfast camping style.
You created a safe world for us amongst
The peaceful breathing mountains.
Traditions constructed where you had not
Experienced in youth.

Love was expressed by your ever present strength
And patience.
Mom said you were a
Good provider. Her only expression
Of value of you.

Your last waking dream was about Uncle David
Coming home on a ship. Excited
To arrange the party for the family.

You are in my heart and
My mind Dad.
I breathe in the grief of missing you.....
And breathe out the joy
Of knowing our next July 4th together will
Be fabulous.

Believe

Won't anyone believe
I can see enough for me.

Be the one to see my soul
Listen to my heart unfold.

Try to stand along with me
As I brave this painful tragedy.

Grieve the loss, grieve the fear
Let yourself inside and disappear.

Let this pain be ours to bear
So that we bravely gather here.

Always seek and you will find
Others' souls to love and bind.

Worth It

I don't know if it's worth it he said.
I have this very expensive thing but all I do is worry
that someone is going to take it.

Profound words.
When you stop and listen.
Words from a man most would never choose to give voice.

Labeled. A lifetime of
Being different with painful
Self-worth missing. Not good enough.

Yet his empathy and compassion
Touch others, at times unexpected and disconcerting.
Softness and need for love
He strives to pray enough. Worried about harsh words spoken describing others.
Lived knowledge of not fitting in.

If we listen
He can be our guide

Silence

What do you hear in the quiet.

What do you feel.

Are you uncomfortable within the stillness.

Needing to fill the calm.

Our thoughts less intrusive if we don't try to listen.

Interested

I am interested.
Create the space, the opening, the moment.

Quiet the intrusions.
Remember to change my face from brooding to smile, sometimes difficult.

As a sponge filters its environment in order to survive
sifting nutrients hoping toxicities that come won't destroy it.

Come positive energy.
Rebuild my soul.
As I try to filter for my survival.

False Dedication

We are called
Compelled in some way to serve those in need

We study and learn our particular skills
to provide care
Dream of the opportunities to improve
and change lives

We identify ourselves as those with a special
calling
Described as Angels who share comfort
during the worst of life

Yet the opportunistic profit driven businesses
condition us and take advantage.
Hiding financial greed under mission statements
mislabeled as non-profits

The reservoir is now empty
Burnout now replacing the compassion and
drive
with numbness and fatigue

There is no more to give

Doctor Niel's Garden

In Scotland the green, sun and rain are one together.

The wind brings the smell of the sea and the green of the hills to the
unsearching.

Dress in layers. On then off, then on again.
Seeking any spot to sit and have the sun kiss as the raindrops wet my face
Like tears from heaven.

You cannot feel the raindrops unless you expose your skin
And yourself.

Difficult Wisdom

Perfectly manicured yard
Routine established, years in the making.

Independence attached to failing health
Daylight and safety allowing self-sufficiency.

The planned or unplanned removal, chink in the structure
Hospitalization and sickness changing the future forever.

In our minds survival never leaves
It just changes as we lose all autonomy
We felt assured.

No wonder the difficult wisdom frequently shared

Don't ever get old.

Edinburgh

Ancient places overwhelmed with tourists
Welcomed to see and experience.

Tales of war and religion
Reasons for destruction and survival.

Proud resilience of the people determined to prevail
Offering their greetings and stories of lived strength.

Honoring the ancients as if connected just yesterday.

Mean Girl

I won't be a mean girl
Loud and demanding to be seen.

Taking words and turning into weapons
Meant to transfer my pain to others.

Smug in my identity of authority
Certain my knowledge is always right.

The wellness of pain and darkness oozing
And exploding beyond my control.

Blinded and unable to feel the reactions
Of those I target.

Blaming others, unable to see
My own brokenness that other try to care for.

Even as I shoot the next arrow.

We Disappear

When I am gone all that is left
are my things that are still
The work and my dreams I was driven to fulfill

She said my friends are gone
and my family too, no one is here
I am so tired with nothing left
I want to lay down and disappear

He sang with friends, they played
and traveled.
His songs bring back the emotions that
reappear as I feel my heart unravel.

Is what we create, whether lasting or
fleeting what is left of our human
imprint of the time we exist
Or perhaps the connections of those we
share emotions whether knowing or unknowing
so that disappearing is no longer pain but a gift.

Self Reliance

Unfettered and assured ability
To decide
From choice of who we wish
To interact with to what we
Injest for need or pleasure.

I knew I should have never
Gotten into the car with that guy
She said. Admitting her
Determined act of self-reliance.

The cruel inevitability of loss
All must experience. Choice and freedoms
In this life.

More than fear of pain or alone-ness
The shaken
Certainty that we can not be independent
Is our greatest worry.

Mom Said

Mom said....see that airplane up
In the sky? I wish
I was on it going anywhere.

Is she finally happy now? The shackles
Of her broken and diseased
Body released.

No longer re-living the
Imbedded memories of her harsh childhood
And fight for a good life.

Always seeking, digging through what
Others discarded sure she
Would find the treasure.

Did she finally know that the
Treasure was always inside her, deep
and hidden. Yet sometimes
Beaming with the love of her grandchildren.

First Love

Painful ecstasy first
experienced with a blind
belief in forever.

Touch of a tender man seeking to
ease the separation from primary love.
Quenching
the grief of forced independence.

Duty, confused independence yet in
reality dependance causing fracture and
end to the dream of an evermore future.

Pain and healing with a deep
felt remembrance of the tenderness.
Youth and dreams forced to mature.

When you look

When you look
Really look
You can see me.
My inside
Self
Fear
Pain
Dreams
Overwhelming need
We are ending
Relationship
Partnership
Dream
Love
Pain

How can I communicate my reality
You ask why
Is there really any way you can understand
That it had to be

To keep me whole
To keep me sane
To keep myself alive
To heal my soul

Minikhada

Pathways found, uncovered from the sandy flood
and
forgotten in time.

Flagstones and smoothed river rock
Stones stacked to tell a tale
Paths leading to secret gardens.

Years harvesting the perfect flat river stones
Hours kneeling to ensure perfect placement.

The paths are again forgotten and unattended
without your care.

What If

It should be so simple we think
Decide what makes you happy and do that.

You shall be happy, content.
Dream big. You can be and do anything you want.

If you didn't get it, your dream,
You must not have wanted it bad enough or worked hard enough.
The failure was yours.

What if as a child we were instead challenged to become honest, loving and kind to others.
If success were to be measured this way what would our world be like?
Less single parent families
Domestic violence
Equitable opportunities and a world view that we are all positively connected.
Seeking happiness for all.

Live the peace
Peace I choose
It is not so easy
When we refuse

Dad Again

Did you make it Dad?
The coming ship you were preparing for your last days here.

You were plan-ful, anticipating what was needed when the ship came
Excited to meet the family who would join the big party.

You seemed happy and relaxed as your body failed.
As if this passage would bring you happiness.

The memory comfort the painful loss of you.
The hope that you joined your ship and crossed into an existence of peace.

Prayer

Do you pray he asked.
Well of course, I think so, how do I know.

I don't think I pray hard enough he said.
Memorized words uttered with sincere intent
Time spent in defined adoration.

Do you pray he asked.
I think so.
What if I define my prayer as the empathy I share
Touch to the troubled
Listening to those without words.

Would I be praying hard enough.

Sadness

The light is hidden when the mist
Of doubt and pain
Seeps into my mind.
Memories and feelings of
Old pain
Fear leak out of the tightly
Closed box I have so diligently secure shut.

Slogging through a dark
And seemingly pointless day brings
Me close to the bursting open
Of my box of pain.
When will the pandemic end
And with it the season of intolerance
And hate.

I remind myself, over
And over even seconds at times
Of what I am grateful for.
As I smile the box closes
Tight again.

Mothers' Conversation

She told me she didn't speak English. Ukraine she said.

I said God Bless You, tapping my heart.

We could not speak the same language but we had a conversation.

I learned she left some of her family behind for this country.
Her son is a soldier in the war now.

We both cried.
She allowed me to embrace her.

We dried our tears and moved forward,
continuing our paths.
As mothers do.

Solitude

Detached space and time
Chosen inadvertently occurring
Shall this be healing or
An unwrapping of remembered ghosts.

The first cup of warm coffee
Of the day. In the quiet of the dog
Snore and view of the awakening birds.

Deep breath seeping warm memories as
I guide my thoughts to gratefulness,
Remember small joys and events when
I was loved.
Safely secluded in my mind to rise when needed.

Isolation created space to
Help me answer the unanswerable
Questions I seek.
Emptying and quieting so my truth can rise.

We Search

Testing of actions based on acceptance of group norms.
Simple appearing complex peer tests for acceptance.

Self-sifting identifying who we fit with
Pre-infused parental codes either adopted
or identified and rejected.

Life presents opportunities to find our tribe
Sometimes multiple tribes.
Do we ever really fit as society changes and we are opened to accept all.

You are my tribe.
I just don't know you yet.

Solo

Choice of presentation from searching years of memories
Shaking hand gripping the pick which tries to slip when emotion is peaking.
Friends, family and strangers not yet friends
Supportive. Grateful.

Projecting sound, words, trying to connect
Messages of protest, hope and thought provoking reality.

Awkward introvert stepping out in fear
Exhausted completion of a dream realized.

A musical poet exposed.

Strength

I did not choose to be this way.
Well maybe I did
Except experiences were my incubator.

Guys are stupid he said.....they don't
Know what to do with a
Strong woman. As if from experience.

Don't mistake the potency of
My visage or approach. The intensity
Of my living comes from
Witnessed and experienced pain.
And my endless seeking of
 Ways to give love.

Light

Gather the sunrays as fast as you can
Radicals of warmth that come unplanned.

The ancients knew the importance of savoring the light
As there has never been a certainty that there would be an end to night.

When we learn that caring and truth are the light
Perhaps we will no longer crave and search for it,
but give ourselves in the darkness of quiet.

Welcome

Welcome guest
To the fest
A time to celebrate.

Bring a friend
And make amends
Before it is too late.

Step into life
Which may include strife
To experience your mind.

Be part of the song
We must all sing along
To keep from going blind.

Call Me Thelma

Loving who I choose bravely
with abandon
breaking free from society's
brainwashing of who
I must be.

Learning to live a life
True to myself. Re-born
Yet sacrificing for
Those I love
Who love me.

Grateful for the Louise's
Joining my path

Soaring free.

About the author

Mary is musical poet masked as a nurse in Portland, Oregon.

You can follow her on Instagram @call.me.thelma.